# THE
# *Archive Photographs*
# SERIES

# HARPENDEN

Church Green, January 1947.

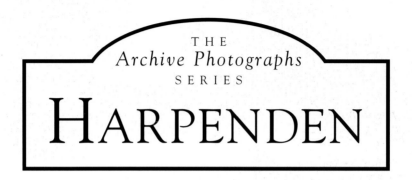

THE
*Archive Photographs*
SERIES

# HARPENDEN

Compiled by
Eric Brandreth

TEMPUS

The Bull Inn signboard, early nineteenth century. This was on display at the Harpenden Fair in 1923. It still exists and is being preserved by the Harpenden Local History Society.

*Dedicated to Sheila and Paul*

First published 1996
Reprinted 2004

Tempus Publishing Limited
The Mill, Brimscombe Port,
Stroud, Gloucestershire, GL5 2QG
www.tempus-publishing.com

British Library Cataloguing in Publication Data.
A catalogue record for this book is available from the British Library.

ISBN 0 7524 0603 5

Typesetting and origination by Tempus Publishing Limited.
Printed in Great Britain.

# Contents

VIEW SHOWING CHURCH.                    Donald F. Merrett

Christmas Greetings.

Church Green, *c.* 1920.

# Introduction

Harpenden is a village situated upon the main road leading from Luton to St Albans, four-and-a-half miles from the latter town. The houses which comprise the village present no uniformity of arrangement but many are well constructed and situated, giving 'the cheerful and engaging appearance for a country residence' described by Pigot's County Directory in 1839.

The population at that time was just under 2,000 and Harpenden was a small agricultural village, with around thirty farms providing the majority of employment.

In 1868 the Midland Railway extended its main line from Bedford to London, giving Harpenden direct communication with the capital. Thirteen years later a large estate was sold, releasing land for housing. A number of local builders acquired areas of varying sizes, and Harpenden's transformation from agricultural village to the commuter town of today had begun. As early as 1895 the *Herts. Advertiser* stated, 'for some time it has been clearly evident that Harpenden has a great future in prospect, and in these days of rapid transmit by train, and the desire of City men to continue the pursuit of wealth with that of health, the oft repeated prediction that Harpenden is destined to become one of London's most valuable suburbs, has already practically become an accomplished fact.' The population did indeed grow rapidly, but not to universal approval. Miss Vaughan, the rector's eldest daughter, spoke for many older inhabitants when she expressed the view in 1893 that she wished Harpenden would soon stop growing, preferring a smaller village in which, 'each knew the other'.

Between 1891 and 1931 the population jumped from nearly 4,000 to just over 9,500. The *Herts. Advertiser* claimed in 1930 that, 'the average Englishman is credited with a keen sense of appreciation of beauty, especially natural scenic beauty. Small wonder, therefore, that Harpenden, which it is agreed on all sides possesses some magnificent natural beauty, has grown enormously during the past six or seven years. In spite of this, however, some inhabitants still call Harpenden a "village" – causing some amusement to newcomers.'

There is much that is charming in retaining this title, despite the fact that Harpenden is still growing very rapidly. Since 1920, 613 houses, thirty-one bungalows and thirty-four shops have been built and as many as twenty new roads have been constructed. The thirties were a time of great expansion; farmlands between the High Street and Lower Luton Road were developed as were the Roundwood and West Common areas. The population in 1939 was estimated to be 13,000. There were also extensive alterations in the village centre – both sides of the High Street, south of Church Green, were largely rebuilt.

Development came to a halt during the war years, but much thought was given to planning for the future. When Professor Patrick Abercrombie published the Greater London Plan in 1944, one of his proposals was for a new satellite town, just west of Redbourn, eventually to accommodate 60,000 people (the proposal was later amended, and Hemel Hempstead was expanded instead). In explaining his choice, Professor Abercrombie wrote that he had surveyed all the towns and villages around London. He described Harpenden as, 'a fairly rapidly expanding middle class residential town on the main London, Midland and Scottish Railway line – train services to London are good. It is essentially a dormitory to London and Luton and, to a lesser degree, to St Albans. The surrounding countryside is attractive, and the town setting is greatly enhanced by the Common, which extends right into the town centre, shops fronting it being set back behind service roads. Communication with Batford and beyond is very bad, owing to lack of bridges over the River Lea; there are two fords and a narrow bridge. The town is not suitable for industry. It is very desirable that Harpenden should retain its present character of compactness, and for this purpose should plan a green belt in its immediate surroundings.' He suggested a population limit of 15,000. The Town Development Plan of 1951 increased this to 20,000. In practice, it is now approaching 30,000.

Changes are inevitable with this scale of growth. The pictures in this book show some of those which have been recorded in the past hundred years or so. I hope you enjoy looking at them as much as I enjoyed choosing them.

# One

# The Common

The Common is Harpenden's pride and joy. Covering 238 acres, it stretches for nearly two miles right into the centre of the town. Over the years its uses have been many and varied. During the last century and the first half of the present one, it was a valuable grazing ground for sheep. One shepherd used to walk his flock there from Batford each day via Crabtree Lane. But the Baa-lamb trees did not get their name from the sheep. Research by Ian Freeman shows that it is a corruption of the family name of Balaam, known in Harpenden for over 300 years. There was a Balaam House on the site of the trees in 1652.

From 1848 until 1914 horse races were held, a week before the Derby. While the races no longer take place, horse riding continues. Cricket, golf and football have been played there for many years. In the late 1930s the North Thames Cross Country Athletic championships were held, with over two hundred competitors. Until the First World War, cottagers grazed their geese and donkeys on the Common, gathered furze and brushwood for their fires, and used it as a drying ground for their laundry.

Entitled, 'The Solitary Rider' when exhibited by Frederick Thurston in 1898. The road is now the A1081, and carries rather more traffic.

Sheep grazing on the common at the turn of the century. The Silver Cup is behind the trees in the centre. Across the road, in front of the Baa-lamb trees, the small tree growing on the island in the Silver Cup pond can just be seen.

A closer view of the natural pond, in a dry period. It was made into a more formal, rectangular pond, with a gently sloping concrete floor in 1899 by Sir John Bennet Lawes, the Lord of the Manor. In 1970 the Urban District Council declared it a potential health risk and had it filled in.

The drainage pond on the Common was created from an old gravel pit in 1928 as part of the Urban District Council's scheme to relieve unemployment. It became an attractive place for an afternoon stroll.

A similar view from the other end of the pond. This area was referred to in some guidebooks of the period as Harpenden's 'little Switzerland'.

Horse races were held on the Common in the spring of every year from 1848 to 1914. The course was in the shape of a big horseshoe from Queens Road to Ayres End and back. The grandstand foundations can be seen, to the left of the trees. It stood roughly where the golf clubhouse is today.

The Grandstand, *c.* 1900. The foundations were left in place but the seating and roof were erected each year by Mr Watler, whose farm was in Queens Road.

At the turn of the century Harpenden had only one policeman. On race day a detachment came to Harpenden from county police headquarters at Hatfield. They travelled on the Great Northern Railway to Batford and marched up to the Common from there. Here they seem to be taking a break before the crowds arrive.

Gypsies were attracted to the races from a wide area around, parking their caravans on many parts of the Common.

A meet of the Hertfordshire hunt on the Common outside the Railway Hotel (now the Harpenden Arms) in 1895. The hunt kennels were built at Kinsbourne Green in 1866. At the outbreak of war, in 1939, the hunt moved to Houghton Regis.

A drumhead service in the same place for soldiers of the Notts. and Derbyshire regiment in the autumn of 1914. Four battalions were billeted in Harpenden at the outbreak of war, to undergo training before going to France.

14

# Two
# Along the High Street

*In the middle of the last century, the High Street was typical of many a small country village. There was a completely unplanned mix of private dwellings, inns, shops (often only one room of the home), farms with slaughterhouses at the rear, and workplaces of various kinds. A small stream ran from the village pond to the Common. Two breweries stood side by side in the street.*

*As the village grew, and good class housing estates were built, the new type of resident required an expanded range of shopping facilities. Some houses were turned into shops, unsuitable buildings were demolished, and workshops were displaced to developing industrial areas.*

The southern end of the High Street in September 1966. The most notable changes from this view are Broadway Hall in the centre, the covered market (replaced by Sainsburys in 1970), the Methodist church gardens where the Davenport House doctors' surgeries were built in 1978 and Anscombes in Leyton Road, demolished in 1983 to make way for Waitrose.

The High Street in 1903 painted by Ernest Hasseldine. Prominent on the right is the Brewery Tower, built in 1897.

This elegant gas lamp standard, seen in the 1930s, marks the junction of the High Street and Station Road. It was not replaced by an electric street light until 1957.

An outing in 1919 – possibly a Peace Day celebration. Note the number of straw hats being worn. The Valley Engineering Company premises became Chirneys Garage in 1920. They were demolished in 1986 and the site is still empty.

The George Hotel in 1920. The stalls on the forecourt are Browns, a greengrocers, and Hammetts, a fishmonger, who came from Luton each day by horse and cart. He opened a shop in the High Street in 1926.

The southern end of the High Street, *c.* 1900. The house next to the George had been the home of Dr Kingston, one of the village doctors. In 1912 Henry Salisbury demolished it and the cottage next door and built his new shop, named Kingston House, for 'household and general furniture'. It is now C&A's.

This end block was built in 1881, following a fire which had destroyed the earlier buildings. The corner building is Marten's Bank, later to become Barclays.

Barclays corner in 1923, showing their new building. In 1956 the bank extended into James Busby's site next door. He moved across the High Street to the shop that is now the Springfield pharmacy.

The buildings between Leyton Green and the White Lion, *c*. 1900. Gibson's Estate Office is now Lloyds Bank. This whole block was redeveloped in 1936 and Lloyds was rebuilt again in 1969.

The shops and houses from the White Lion to Church Green were built in the early 1890s, replacing a large house and walled garden which fronted the Green.

On Tuesday 26 October 1948, eleven years before the M1 opened, this seventy-ton boiler was taken from London to Lancaster. Hauled by two lorries it was 146 feet long.

Looking south towards the Common in the early years of this century, before the roads were tarred and pavements laid. The trees were not removed until 1935.

Church Green, *c.* 1910. There has been an inn on the site of the Old Cock Inn, seen on the right, since the seventeenth century. Behind the road across the Green is the Methodist church in Leyton Road.

The seventeenth-century cottages facing Church Green, seen here in the 1930s, were demolished, after a great deal of controversy, in 1959 and replaced by a supermarket and shops.

The temporary Roman Catholic church in Rothamsted Avenue opened on 28 May 1905 and was in use until 20 October 1929 when the present church was opened by Cardinal Bourne.

St Nicholas School was built in 1864. The seventeenth-century cottages stood beside the entrance to the parish church before they were demolished in 1912. Between them is the Rector's Room, built in 1885 as a much needed classroom and church hall.

Class 2 of St Nicholas School in 1911.

The old parish church of St Nicholas, seen from the north, *c*. 1860. When Canon Vaughan arrived in 1860 as Harpenden's first rector, the church was in a very bad state of repair. After much discussion it was decided to demolish the Norman building, with the exception of the fifteenth-century tower, and rebuild. The new church was reconsecrated on 7 November 1862.

Church Green on Wednesday 19 July 1893. Harpenden celebrated the Rothamsted Golden Jubilee year with a grand fête. The procession of ten fire engines from towns and villages round about, led by the Luton Red Cross Band, was en route to Rothamsted Park for a grand fire brigade competition.

A quieter scene in the same spot, around 1900. Workmen are cleaning the stream which ran from the Cock pond to the Common (see p.38).

A similar view from thirty years later. In the thirties there were no road markings, no bollards, no yellow lines and not much traffic.

The High Street and the Cock pond, *c.* 1880, looking north.

The hut next to Dickinson and Adams garage is Thurston's photography studio, seen in 1953. Frederick Thurston's main business was in Luton and he opened a Harpenden branch overlooking Church Green in 1896, but by 1900 had moved into these premises. He took several of the early photographs reproduced in this book. In 1955 this building was demolished and incorporated into the garage site which is now a Kwikfit centre.

The northern end of the High Street in the 1930s. Kirkwick nurseries closed in 1943 because of wartime conditions. It was an electricians until 1988 when Mr J. Ryan retired.

The shop stood empty for a couple of years, until a Chinese take-away was built on the site. Lots of Rice opened in April 1991.

Across the road, behind the trees, is a row of seventeenth-century cottages, seen here in 1930. The entrance to Sun Lane is just visible on the left, between the wall and the fence.

The part of the cottage, seen in the previous picture, left of the chimney, which was removed in December 1930 when Sun Lane was widened as part of a general traffic improvement scheme. The remainder of the building is now Allsopp's estate agents.

Taken in 1900, this is almost the same scene as the picture opposite, with the trees lopped. The house with the porch was the home of Captain Arthur Lydekker, the first chairman of the Urban District Council.

Standing out in the roadway, this cottage was often referred to as Toll Gate Cottage. There was a toll road through Harpenden from 1743 to 1879 but the actual gate was further up the road. The cottage was demolished in 1930, shortly after this photograph was taken.

In the centre is Lines blacksmith's shop, *c*. 1925. It was built in 1820 and closed in 1957 after being worked by three generations of the Lines family. The forge, and the private houses on each side of it, were demolished in 1960 and the appropriately named Anvil House built on the site. On the extreme left of the picture is the cottage which can seen on page 29.

The Foresters Arms, *c*. 1938. There was an earlier Foresters Arms on this site in the last century, popularly known as Cobweb Hall. It was rebuilt in 1907 as seen here. It closed in 1960 and is now Wine Rack off licence.

Bowers House and the Cock pond, c. 1895. The house dates from the sixteenth century. From 1850 it had been the home of Dr Frederick Spackman and his family. After his death, in 1892, his daughter, Alice, ran a school for around forty girls there for some years.

Taken at the same time as the previous picture, we see Pollards, the tall eighteenth-century house on the left, which was a private home until 1918. It then became the Harpenden School of Music until 1946. Next door is the Cross Keys which has been an inn for at least 250 years.

The Cock pond site in 1930. The pond was filled in in 1928, and a small park laid out. Bowers Parade was built across Bowers House gardens in 1936. Two years later the old cottages seen between the trees were removed, and Reads motor showrooms were built as an extension to the Parade.

A view from the turn of the century. The building to the left of Thompsons Close, a private house at this time, was the Fisher, Knight printing works in 1919. Later it became the gas showrooms for many years, and is now Lunn Poly. The shop with the blind is Oliver Jewers, linen draper and boot factor. He had occupied the site since 1874, when the whole building was known as Rose Cottage. It is now The Studio.

Thompsons Close in 1897. The tall house is Pollards (seen on p.31). Thompsons Close, popularly known as Vinegar Lane for reasons which are now obscure, was an ancient pathway from the village to Batford.

The Lower High Street has always been prone to flooding following heavy rain such as here, on 13 August 1937. The shops were demolished in 1968 and are now replaced by the Woolwich and the Abbey National.

In the middle of the last century, there were two breweries in the High Street. The owners' houses stood side by side, with the brewery buildings behind them. This is Peacock House in around 1870, a year before Mr Mardall had it taken down. In 1893 Mardalls bought Healey's brewery and concentrated the workings on one site.

Peacock House was quickly replaced by this one, known as Brewery House and inhabited until 1951 when it was sold to become commercial premises. It is now W.H. Smiths and Going Places.

An painting from around 1860 of The White House, home of Jack Healey, owner of the other brewery. The road across the immediate foreground is Leyton Road while the buildings on the right are the ones which burnt down in 1880, to be replaced by those seen on page 18 at Barclays corner.

The White House was pulled down in the late 1920s and the new High Street Methodist church erected on its land by Mr A. Harris and Son, local builders.

The new Methodist church in 1930. The notice-board is announcing its opening services, which took place on 17 September.

Mrs Mardall sold the combined brewery to Richard Glover in 1897. He modernised the buildings and erected the tower. In 1919 the brewery closed, and became Waverley sportswear mills. Waverley mills moved to the old cinema building in Leyton Green in 1936 and this complex was sold, and the buildings demolished to be replaced by Boots, Sainsburys and Woolworths.

Mr George Bevins, owner of Waverley mills, in his office in 1923. Note his magnificent telephone – it was number 21. There were 188 subscribers at this time, in a population of nearly 7,000.

This is the handworkers' room of the firm, which made knitted goods.

The winding room.

The stream from the Cock pond flowing along the Lower High Street in 1913. The White House (see p.35) is just off the picture to the left. Sometimes grandly referred to as the River Harp, the stream was dependant on rain water. (see p.33 for a contrasting scene).

The scouring room.

W. Pellant and Sons, watchmakers and jewellers, on the corner of the High Street and Vaughan Road in around 1899, a year or two after the building was erected. It is now Felicitations.

Harridens, *c.* 1970. The shop was built in the late 1890s with some rather nice decorative work around the windows and on the gable. It became Harridens in 1922.

The interior seen in the mid 1930s. They had a coffee grinding machine, which produced a beautiful aroma around the shop. Harridens closed in 1975. The shop is now Perrys florists.

# Three

# Southdown

This area was originally known as Bowling Alley. The name comes not from the game, but from the shape of a field. In 1784 there were two fields, Upper and Lower Bowling Alley which were later combined before Longfield Road was built over them.

Before the arrival of the railway, Bowling Alley consisted of three or four houses on the eastern side of the road and an almost continuous row of houses from the Queens Head to the Rose and Crown on the other. As the track approached, some of those standing in the way of the embankment were demolished. The train company had bought land from Limbrick Farm and when the line was completed surplus land was sold for houses, precipitating Bowling Alley's growth. There were forty-eight houses in 1861 and ten years later another ninety-eight had been built, in Cravells Road and Grove Road. The latest part of this development process was as recent as 1988, when a strip of land between Walkers Road and Cravells Road behind St John's church was sold by British Rail.

Skew Bridge was built in 1865 with two tracks which were doubled in 1891. Note the temporary track at road level, for the delivery of materials.

The sixteenth-century Harpenden Hall has been many things in its lifetime: private house, boys' grammar school, private lunatic asylum, girls' boarding school (twice) and, latterly, offices of the Urban District Council. Here, in 1924, it is the St Dominic's Convent School. The garden in the foreground is where the Public Hall was built in 1938.

Over the wall to the left is Station Road. Where the greenhouse and small group of girls stand is now the Public Hall car park.

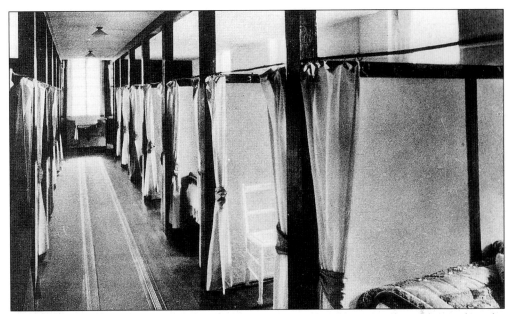

St Dominic's Senior Girls' Dormitory. The school moved a short way down the road to the Welcombe (now the Moat House) in 1931, and Harpenden Hall became the Urban District Council offices.

From 1910 until 1923 Harpenden Hall was a girls' school run by Miss English, with accommodation for twenty girls. The fees for residence and general education were £35 per term, with an extra five shillings for games. Here on Peace Day, Saturday 19 July 1919, the girls are setting off for a picnic at Gustard Wood.

A cricket match on the Common around 1890. The meadow over the road was part of the Welcombe estate, owned by Mr Henry Tylston Hodgson, Deputy Chairman of the Midland Railway. It was sold for development in 1934. The houses on the horizon are in Milton Road.

Lower Topstreet Farm at the corner of Crabtree Lane and Topstreet Way in 1880. It ceased to be a farm in 1924 – the barns were pulled down and the farm pond filled in. The house still stands however.

St John's church hall, *c.* 1908. It was built for the church by Mr Hodgson in 1906. On New Year's Eve 1905, the first St John's, on the corner of Crabtree Lane, was burnt down, so, from its opening in March, this hall was also used for church services. In 1967 it was sold to the Harpenden Trust.

Children of the St John's National School at Southdown celebrating Empire Day around 1911. The Rose and Crown is on the extreme right.

Bowling Alley in the 1880s. The small building on the right is Charles Ogglesby's blacksmith's shop which began business in 1873. Towards the end of the century the firm started to repair bicycles. Charles died in 1912 and his son, Frederick, began making bicycles to order, as well as repairing them. In 1923 the forge was transferred to the corner of Walkers Road, and this site became a motor garage.

The forge in 1916. Frederick Ogglesby is fifth from the left, standing beside the little boy.

The Primitive Methodist church at Southdown, built in 1865. The building is still there, although a new front has been added on three occasions: in 1899, 1959 and 1970.

The Church Hall around 1970. It was erected for the Sunday school in 1899. In 1979 the hall was taken down, and Finefare supermarket built there, with church rooms on the first floor. The supermarket is now Somerfields.

Fred Timson standing beside his cobbler's shop at the corner of Cravells Road and Southdown Road during the First World War. The left hand window is decorated as a roll of honour to the men of South Harpenden.

At the corner of his garden, Fred Timson maintained this shrine for some years. The two outer columns contain the names of those serving, and the centre column is a list of the fallen.

Cravells Road in the 1890s. The last block of houses on the right, just behind the Carpenters Arms pub sign, was demolished around 1961, and the site is now a car park. Just beyond the first lamp-post is the entrance of Abraham Saunders removal business, opened in 1894. It is now Tylers' motor workshops.

Twenty-five prefabs were erected in Grove Road in 1946. They remained until 1964 when houses in what is now Oakley Road replaced them.

During 1930 Piggottshill Lane was widened to cater for the increasing motor traffic. This tree was felled on 20 May and a small crowd turned out to witness the event.

Grove Road pond in the 1930s. A gravel pit in the last century, it became a reservoir for the Millwall Rubber Company, which stood nearby.

Now a drainage pond, tucked away in a corner of the civic amenities dump in Dark Lane, it is seen here being cleaned out in September 1936.

When the first St John's church was burnt down, on the last day of 1905, the congregation immediately started raising funds for a new building. The foundation stone was laid in July 1907 on a site given by Sir Charles Lawes-Wittewronge. Seen here, later in the year, the contractors, Phillips and Blake, are making good progress. The man wearing a straw hat is the rector, the Revd Andrew Keogh.

ST. JOHN'S CHURCH, HARPENDEN. 28.

The new St John's church was consecrated on 2 March 1908 by the Bishop of St Albans. The total building costs were £3,300.

## Four

# West Common and Leyton Road

*West Common and Leyton Road occupy an important site on the edge of the Common. The Harpenden Conservation Area Plan, published in 1973, included this area. The Plan asserted that 'building along the fringes of the Common has always had a maximum visual impact, from the elaborate neo-Georgian style of Rothamsted Laboratory to the more intimate scale of the Pimlico cottages'. It acknowledged that a consistency of natural materials of brick, stone and timber had been upheld and recommended that this should be followed in any new development. The sixteen terraced cottages of Pimlico Place were built in 1822 by the Benefit and Annuitant Society of St Albans, of whom little is known. The laboratory building was completed during the First World War and there have been extensive developments on the land behind since then.*

The Elms in Leyton Road around 1930, complementing the Baa-lamb trees on the left. They suffered badly from Dutch Elm disease and were felled in the early eighties.

Hatching Green, c. 1880. The main entrance to Rothamsted Manor, home of Sir John Bennet Lawes and his family, is through the gates between the hedge and the wall.

This imposing piece of statuary is in the Manor grounds. It was created by Sir Charles Lawes-Wittewronge in 1908, entitled Death of Dirce. Dirce, in Greek legend, was the second wife of Lycus, King of Thebes. She persecuted his first wife, Antiope. To avenge their mother, Antiope's twin sons tied Dirce to a bull and left her to die.

Flowton Priory was built in 1525 at Flowton, near Ipswich, as a Priory House. In the 1920s it had deteriorated and was being used as a granary. A St Albans resident saw it, thought it worth preserving, and bought it. It was completely dismantled and stored for some years while a suitable site was sought.

Eventually one was found at West Common. The materials were packed under the architect's direction and transported the eighty-six miles to Harpenden by road. The house was rebuilt on its present site by Mr J. Dennis, a St Albans builder, to the exact pattern of the original, and completed in 1928.

The Rothamsted Testimonial Laboratory was built in 1855. Farmers nation-wide contributed to a building fund in appreciation of the benefits Lawes' and Gilbert's experiments were bringing them. It was in use until 1913 when the present laboratory replaced it.

An interior view. Miss Winifred Brenchley was appointed in 1906, the first woman on the staff at Rothamsted. She was responsible for all the botanical work, including sorting of different grasses. After her appointment, girls were employed to do the sorting, which for the previous sixty years had been done by boys.

Rothamsted in 1956 showing the extensive allotments. In 1852, in a time of rural hardship, John Bennet Lawes had put aside ten acres of land to provide allotments for the agricultural labourers of the parish. Five years later he built them a clubhouse, seen in the centre, where they could have their beer and tobacco in more comfort than was possible, 'in the limited accommodation of the labourer's cottage, where the small fire is entirely surrounded by his wife and children.' The club was a great success, and another ten acres of land were provided. In 1859 Charles Dickens visited it and published an article about it in his periodical, *All the Year Round*. The allotment club flourished for over a hundred years. However, in 1965 Jack Underhill, who had been the steward for thirty years, died and no-one could be found to take over the responsibilities of running the club leading to its disbandment in September 1967. New buildings now cover most of the area.

Rivers Lodge, the home of Thomas Wilson and his family. The main part of the house dates from the early eighteenth century. The extension on the right was designed by his son Denis, an architect, and built in 1914. The house is now part of the Rothamsted buildings.

The fire station on Christmas Day 1991 – the only day in the year when it is possible to get a view unobstructed by parked cars. The fire brigade had been there since 1901. The building was shortly to be demolished, to make a roadway through to James Marshall House and the Day Centre.

Seen on 31 March 1991, this site had been the Harpenden garden centre for some years. It is now the home of the new fire station, which opened in September 1992.

Preparing the ground for the fire station foundations in April 1991.

Leyton Road in the early years of this century. The lady is standing at the entrance to Bennets, which had, in those days, a covered verandah from the gate to its door.

A similar view around sixty years later. The Elms suffered from Dutch Elm disease and were felled in the early eighties.

Looking towards Leyton Green, *c.* 1910. The building on the right is at the back of the George Hotel and the building on the left is Salisbury's cycle depot, now the site of the Inn on the Green.

Leyton House, on Leyton Green, *c.* 1900, at this time the home of Dr Blake. From 1924 untill 1927 it was St Vincent's Hostel for Boys, a probationary home for youths remanded by London magistrates, the first such Catholic hostel in the country.

The eighteenth-century Wellington House in 1984, undergoing extensive restoration. It is now the Aldwickbury Housing Association offices.

Anscombe's department store on an early Sunday morning in the late 1970s. The firm started in Rose Cottage in 1855 (see p.32), transferred to Wellington House in 1874, and over the years extended along Leyton Road. It closed in 1982, to be replaced by Waitrose.

The rapid wire cash system, by which the counter assistants sent money to the central cash desk in the wooden containers – one is arriving at the left.

Each doorway had one of these mosaic doorsteps.

The first Methodist church services in Harpenden were held in 1792 in two ancient cottages on West Common, now the site of Red Gables. They were demolished in 1902.

The cottages became too small for the increasing congregation, and this chapel, in Leyton Road, was built in 1839. Services were held there for the next forty-seven years.

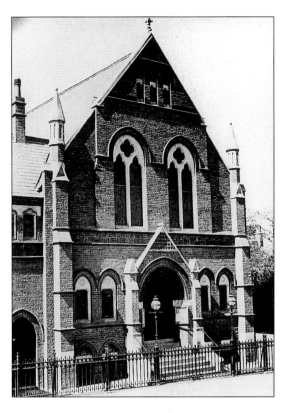

A new building was erected on the same site in 1886. This closed in 1930 when the new High Street premises opened. It became the Regent Cinema, then Anscombe's furniture department and now provides the site for the northern end of the Waitrose supermarket.

Interior of the 1886 chapel. The two stained glass windows, designed by James Salisbury, were transferred to the new High Street Methodist church, and are now in the lecture hall there.

Leyton Green in the 1930s. Leyton House is on the left and to the right of the tree is Hazelbank House.

Hazelbank House stood in a large garden behind Anscombe's before it was taken down in 1983. Its enlarged driveway is now the entrance to the Waitrose car park, which has replaced the garden.

# Five

# Luton Road to Kinsbourne Green

*Canon Vaughan, Harpenden's first rector, arrived in 1860. A rectory was being prepared for him, along the Luton Road, in what were then green fields and is now Old Rectory Close. There were no buildings between there and Kinsbourne Green apart from the small farm of Moreton End, and the Old Bell, to which one cottage was attached. The Nickey Line bridge was not built until 1877.*

*Kinsbourne Green was a relatively remote hamlet, clustered around the Common. The name Kinsbourne is of Saxon origin, thought to mean Cyne's burial place. The medieval manor of Kinsbourne Hall was second only to Rothamsted in importance. In 1254 it belonged to Roger De Kynnesbourne. In 1401 it was bought by William Annabull of Dunstable and for many years the name of the property alternated between the two. It is now known as Annables, the present building dating from the eighteenth century.*

Luton Road at Kinsbourne Green, c. 1925, looking towards Harpenden. St Mary's church is on the right.

Harpenden Lodge, built in 1804, and the home of the Lydekker family for 130 years, seen from its park in 1981.

Looking from the house. The house and park were sold in 1981 and all the land beyond the railings has been developed with high class housing, the Lydekker Park Estate.

The Lodge sitting room around 1880.

There were several decorated doors like this one, seen here in 1981.

The Embassy cinema opened on 27 November 1935. It closed due to falling attendances on 30 October 1983, a few days after this picture was taken.

The foyer, with the hot dog stand beside the stairs.

The auditorium from the balcony.

When the Embassy closed, Ogglesbys demolished it and extended their garage on to the site. This was the scene in August 1984.

The Nickey Line between Harpenden and Hemel Hempstead which opened in 1877 and closed to passenger traffic in 1947. Roundwood Halt was opened in 1927, to serve residents of the estate which was being developed there. The houses are at the top of Moreton End Lane. There was a footbridge across the line just behind us.

In 1929 a bus service started between Harpenden and Boxmoor in competition with the Nickey. In response, this Ro-Railer with interchangeable road and rail wheels was introduced as an experiment, but it was discontinued after a couple of years. It had seating accommodation for twenty-six passengers. It is seen here in January 1931.

The Old Bell was a farm in the middle of the last century. It became a public house in 1873. It has been extended twice, in 1905 and 1960, and then modernised in 1972. This picture dates from the 1920s.

The small engineering factory on the corner of Luton Road and Roundwood Lane was built in 1937. It was known as the Cedardale works when it closed in 1984. The much larger Homedell retirement homes opened there in 1986.

Cooters End Farm seen from
Ambrose Lane in December 1957.
The trees fell victim to Dutch Elm
disease in the late seventies and
have been felled.

A closer view of the farmhouse in
1957. It became dilapidated and
was practically rebuilt in 1970.

Roundwood Lane at its junction with Luton Road in around 1959. The road which curves across the picture is Park Rise. The houses being built are in Park Rise Close, which is about to be extended through the wooded area to join up with Harpenden Rise, just off the picture. The factory site (see p.73) has now been covered by the Homedell Housing Association block and the Bethesda Home. The Roundwood Schools can be seen in the top left hand corner.

The Sanatorium, part of the National Children's Home and Orphanage, was built on high ground in the north-east of Harpenden. It opened in June 1910 for children with tuberculosis – fresh air playing an important part in their treatment. This photograph was taken soon after.

NATIONAL CHILDREN'S HOME, THE DISPENSARY, THE SANATORIUM, HARPENDEN.

The well stocked pharmacy around the same time.

In 1913 the Bonner Road, London, branch of the Home was transferred to Harpenden. The Home, in Ambrose Lane, became practically self-contained. There was a large grass oval in the centre, seperating the girls' houses to the left of the entrance and the boys' to the right. Straight ahead were the administrative offices, school and workshops. This picture was taken in the mid-twenties.

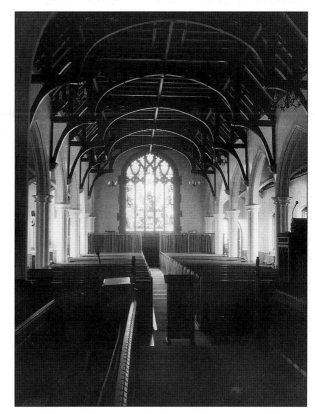

In 1928 the temporary chapel was replaced by this beautiful building, erected by Mr A. Harris, a local builder. The stained glass window was designed by Mr Frank O. Salisbury, the world famous artist.

From the early days the Home was providing its children with a good training for their adult lives. The annual report for 1915 proudly announced that 'the printing works are amongst the best equipped and most modern of such buildings. Twenty-five of the senior boys are apprenticed as compositors and machinists.' Other boys were taught carpentry, engineering, bootmaking or tailoring.

'Most of the girls are prepared for domestic service. In the kitchen, the laundry and the sewing room each girl has a period of training to fit her to take a suitable situation at the age of sixteen,' remarked the same document. Some of the girls were trained in shorthand, typewriting and book-keeping. A few girls and boys were selected to be pupil teachers.

A classroom at the sanatorium, where as much work as possible was done in the open air, including the physical training lessons.

The National Children's Home depended upon voluntary donations for its funds. To ensure public awareness of its work, it issued many sets of postcards. This is number thirty-one, entitled 'a pyramid of happy children at Harpenden.'

Luton Road on Monday 16 September 1968. The house on the right is number 365, now the Icknield veterinary surgery. Despite strenuous attempts to prevent it, the Luton Road has long been prone to flooding after very heavy rain. On this occasion more than an average month's rain had fallen in eighteen hours. In some places the water was two feet deep and took all day to clear.

Green Lawns was built in the early thirties as a small country club. It had a petrol station, restaurant, tennis court and putting green, and attracted a large, well-to-do clientele. Across the road is the Harrow which occupied the site since the middle of the last century. Extended in 1980, it re-opened as a Beefeater restaurant.

In the early fifties Harpenden had the reputation of having a large proportion of unmade roads. The Close was one of them – it was made up in the mid-sixties. When the houses were built in the thirties a new St Mary's church was planned for the centre. After the war however the land was sold, bungalows were built on it, and the existing church was enlarged.

The Fox, c. 1925. There has been an inn here since the eighteenth century. From the early nineteenth century it was owned by Roberts and Wilson, who were brewers at Ivinghoe before they were taken over by Benskins in 1927. The building had a large extension in 1987.

The communal water pump on Luton Road, c. 1910. The building behind is the old Methodist church which was rebuilt in 1951. There had been a well here for many years but the hand operated pump was not installed until 1905, at a cost of £90.

Water at Annables Farm, at the top of Kinsbourne Green, came from a well, 145 foot deep. The donkey raised the bucket, which held eighteen gallons, by walking the wheel. It took about fifteen minutes with a full load. In 1900 the donkey, called Dink, was retired when a mechanical pump was installed.

# Six

# Station Road to Batford

*Harpenden had its origins at Batford. The first settlers were the Belgae, who came up the River Lea which was deeper and wider then, in the first century BC. They created small settlements in the area, of which traces were unearthed in the last century, on the site of Harpenden East railway station, now the site of Waveney Road. 2,000 years later, at the beginning of this century, Batford was a small hamlet on the eastern side of the River Lea. There was a bridge at Pickford and a ford at Westfield, linking it with Coldharbour. The cottagers grew watercress in beds alongside the Lea and made baskets from osiers (willow) grown along the banks to pack it in. There were extensive glasshouses in the valley which produced salad crops and flowers for the London market. The river had a plentiful supply of crayfish and fishing for these was a popular activity in the thirties. Yet in 1945 the Greater London Plan said Batford needed tidying up. The Lea Valley Group was formed in 1971 to do just that. They reconstructed a broken weir, restored a large pool to its former glory, and created a riverside walk, which has transformed the area.*

The Batford and Manland area in September 1959. The glasshouses are conspicuous on the left. They were demolished in 1959 and provided the site for Wroxham Way and Oulton Rise. The houses at Batford were mostly built during the fifties. The field opposite Manland School (now Sir John Lawes School) is now Manland Way.

Ridleys' ironmongery shop at the corner of Station Road, seen just after its construction in 1897. It was acquired by the Midland Bank in 1933. At the top of the road, is the old cottage seen in the next picture.

Station Road in 1896. At the bottom of the road, on the right, is Chestnut Cottage which was demolished to make way for Ridleys. The old cottage and barn were replaced by Hardings (see p.85) which was built when Victoria Road was made.

Station Road in the early years of the century, possibly celebrating the return of soldiers from the Boer War. The thatched cottage half-way up the road stands where the new post office was built in 1928.

Robert Harding's new office block replaced an old cottage (see p.84). He was an estate agent and auctioneer there for nearly forty years. Harding Parade, the block of shops built in 1963 on the opposite side of Station Road, was named in his honour. This building is now the fish and chip shop.

Harpenden station and station-master's house, c. 1935. The Midland Railway's Bedford to London extension came through Harpenden in 1868. The station-master's house was built then, at a cost of £475, and demolished in 1988 after standing empty for many years. It had a very attractive garden, alongside Station Approach.

Douglas Lovatt, the last station-master to live in the house, watching the installation of this improved destination board in August 1962 which was itself replaced by a computerised model in 1982.

Approaching Harpenden station from the north in 1895. The house immediately above the engine is the Red House in Carlton Road, now the Memorial Hospital.

Harpenden station in 1981. The old footbridge, ahead, is being replaced by a new one.

The Red House was built in 1892 as a private home for Mr Vaughan Stevens, a London business man.

It burnt down in August 1896 while the family were away on holiday. The fire is believed to have been caused by a fault in the electric generator.

The house was rebuilt in a slightly more plain style. In 1904 it was bought by Sir Halley Stewart, chairman of the London Brick Company. This is the entrance hall during his early years there. In 1930, he gave the building to the people of Harpenden for use as a hospital after his death. He died in 1937 and despite wartime difficulties the hospital opened in 1941.

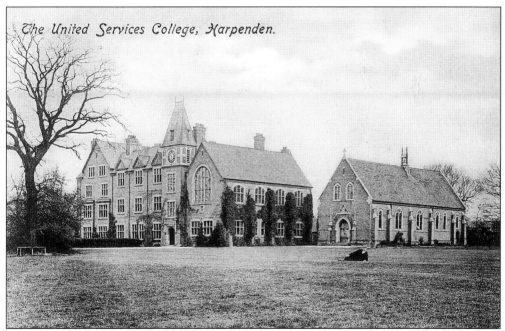

St George's School in 1905. It was built in 1896, for the Revd R.H. Wix, as a boarding school for 100 boys. This first St George's closed in 1904. For two years the buildings were occupied by a branch of the United Services College from Westward Ho. The present St George's opened in June 1907, having transferred from Keswick.

Looking south-west from the top of the water tower in Shakespeare Road towards the Common in the mid 1950s. The bowling green in the centre is in Spenser Road.

The Harpenden Bowling Club was formed in 1908 with its green in Spenser Road on the site of an old tennis court, and is still there. This picture is from around 1953.

From the top of the water tower in 1936, looking just north of west. Shakespeare Road runs diagonally from bottom right to top left. The water company was founded in 1885. For a short period during the thirties there were three storage towers but only one remains, the others replaced by a large underground reservoir.

The post office at the Batford end of Station Road, near the Great Northern Railway bridge, c.1920. The post office is still there but the railway closed in April 1965.

Driver's eye view at Harpenden East station in 1965. Harpenden's first railway was a branch of the Great Northern from Hatfield to Luton, which came through Batford in 1860.

A similar view a few weeks later – the line closed on 24 April 1965. Waveney Road has since been built along the route of the line.

Pickford Bridge at the turn of the century. The building on the left is the Great Northern Railway goods shed. Until Westfield Road bridge was built, in 1964, this was the only bridge across the River Lea between East Hyde and Leasey Bridge.

Taken just after the bridge was rebuilt in 1921. A tubular bridge for pedestrians was installed alongside it in the early fifties. This bridge was itself rebuilt in August 1996.

The view from the bridge around 1938. The building ahead is Pickford Mill which was a paper mill for a century since 1750. It then served as a flour mill until 1897 when Mr Vaughan Stevens converted it into a gutta-percha factory. Gutta-percha is a rubbery latex, once used in the manufacture of golf balls. It was also used in electrical insulation, which may be why Vaughan Stevens was involved. His residence, the Red House, had been burnt down the year before because of an electrical fault (see p.88). The Almagam Rubber Company took over from 1911.

The first All Saints church in Coldharbour Lane in 1909. It was built in 1889 and demolished in 1965 when the new church was opened on Station Road, near Pickford Corner.

The Urban District Council sewage works in Piggottshill Lane in 1930 after large scale extensions which were necessitated by the huge population expansion since their erection in 1911. The houses at the top of the picture are in Batford Road.

The prisoner of war camp off Common Lane was opened in 1943 and held just under 1,000 people. The last prisoners were repatriated in March 1948 and the camp was then adapted for civilian housing accommodation to help meet the desperate shortage.

A German prisoner of war clearing snow in the High Street under a watchful eye in January 1945.

Part of the camp was renovated in 1948 to become a hostel for agricultural workers. The remaining twenty-five huts were converted into fifty, admittedly rather small, homes. These pictures of the empty camp were taken in March 1948.

The site was eventually used for permanent housing, now Milford Hill. While foundations were being dug, in 1957, this tunnel was discovered. At first it was thought that it might have been a potential escape tunnel, but after examination it seemed more likely to have been used many years earlier for digging chalk to mix with the soil, a common agricultural practice in these parts.

Hyde View Road under construction in September 1928. The road in the background is St James Road.

Four-and-a-half months later, in February 1929, the builders have made good progress.

# Seven

# Vaughan Road

*Polly Nott's sweet shop in the High Street was demolished in the mid 1890s to allow the land between the High Street and the railway line to be developed. Vaughan Road and Victoria Road (leading from Station Road) met at right angles. The board school, the police station, and the Congregational church were built on three of the corners. The field on which the church stands used to house a travelling circus which paid regular visits to the village. Vaughan Road was named to commemorate Canon Edward Thomas Vaughan, Harpenden's first rector. He retired in 1896 at the age of eighty-three, moved to Worthing, and died there four years later.*

Brewery Meadow, between Vaughan Road and Bowers Way, seen beyond the gate, in 1960. The two were not connected until 1961 when this land, the remnant of the old Brewery estate, was needed for future use as a car park.

Kingston House lawn-mower showrooms, newly built in 1938, with its workshops next door. The firm moved to Southdown in 1978, and this building became Penden Fair. In 1989 a third storey was added, and the frontage completely reclad. It is now a delicatessen.

The workshops in the thirties – they transferred to the newly developed industrial estate at Skew Bridge in 1965. This building was demolished and a block of shops, with offices above, was built there.

Harpenden Auto Services garage in 1980. The building on the left is the police station. The business moved to Sandridge in June 1981 and, along with the houses on the right, it was demolished to make way for Parkinson House.

Charlie's Auction Rooms in 1982. This corrugated iron hut had been erected in 1901 as a gymnasium. During the thirties it was a school of dancing and elocution but it was demolished in 1983. Charles House, which matches Parkinson House, stands there now.

Across the road were the Victoria Road Schools, seen around 1938. They were built in 1896 to replace the old British School buildings which are now Park Hall. An extension was built across the playground in 1964 to provide more room for the public library.

A school class in 1911.

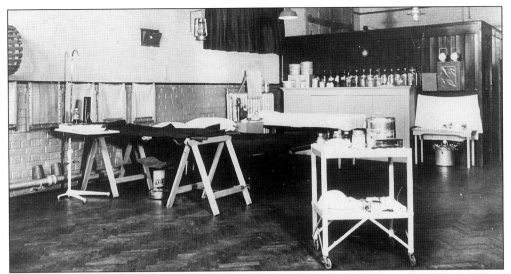

In 1939 the children transferred from Victoria Road to the newly built school at Manland (now Sir John Lawes), and these buildings became a first aid post staffed continuously for the duration of the war by the Red Cross. This is a corner of the emergency treatment room.

In 1947 the northern end of the building became the public library, seen here in 1962, a couple of years before its much needed extension. Note the card catalogue and the manual loan recording system – this was twenty-four years before the computer was installed.

103

# Harpenden
# County Council Schools
### Victoria Road

# EVENING CLASSES

### SESSION 1919-20
#### Commencing
# Monday, October 6, 1919

### COURSE I

| | |
|---|---|
| *Shorthand* . . . . | *Mondays 7-9 p.m.* |
| *Commercial Correspondence & Book-keeping* | *Thursdays 7-9 p.m* |

### COURSE II

| | |
|---|---|
| *Woodwork and Metalwork* . | *Tuesdays & Fridays 7.30-9.30 p.m.* |
| *Practical Drawing and Workshop Arithmetic* | *Wednesdays 7-9 p.m.* |

### COURSE III

| | |
|---|---|
| *Household Cookery* . . | *Tuesdays 7-9 p.m.* |

### FEES FOR THE SESSION
#### (Payable in advance)

| | |
|---|---|
| Students educated at a Public Elementary School ... ... ... | 2/- per Course |
| Others ... ... ... ... | 4/- per Course |

*Intending Students should register on Monday, October 6, between the hours of 6 p.m. and 7 p.m. at the Schools.*

JEFFERY. PRINTER. HARPENDEN

The evening class programme for 1919. We have more choice nowadays.

# *Eight*
# Farming

A hundred and fifty years ago there were about thirty farms of varying sizes in Harpenden. This area was famous for its wheat, the abundance of which gave rise to the straw plait trade, based in Luton and Dunstable. The 1951 County Development Plan described Harpenden as a mixed farming area, of arable and dairy farms, including apple and cherry orchards as recent innovations. One local farmer recalls the changes of the past fifty years as being a general change from livestock to arable and the effective end of horse power. As the town has developed, much farmland has been sold for housing estates. In 1850 over half of Harpenden's working population was involved in farming. In 1991 the figure is less than one per cent. Now over half the working population are commuters.

William Smith in 1947 ploughing at Mr W.S. Piggott's Thrales End Farm, where he had worked since 1926.

Bringing in the hay at Thrales End Farm in the late 1940s. William Smith is leading the white horse.

Edwin Grey, Field Superintendent at Rothamsted for many years, demonstrating the smock, traditionally worn by almost all farm workers in the last half of the nineteenth century. Edwin Grey published, *Cottage Life in a Hertfordshire Village* (i.e. Harpenden), in 1934. It is a very readable account of 'how the agricultural labourer lived and fared in the late 1860s and 70s.'

A reaper binder at work around 1900 on land in the Lea Valley, part of Topstreet Farm. This is now the Aldwickbury Crescent area.

Following the binder and stooking the sheaves to dry. The Great Northern Railway runs across the picture. Its bridge over Piggottshill Lane is just visible on the right, on the edge of the cornfield.

Threshing the corn with flails around 1890, before the widespread distribution of threshing machines which had been introduced at the Great Exhibition of 1851. Flailing required a great deal of skill: an inexperienced user could easily give himself a nasty knock.

Under the direction of the Hertfordshire War Agricultural Executive Committee eighty acres of Harpenden Common were ploughed for cultivation during the Second World War. The golf clubhouse at Hammonds End was also requisitioned as a hostel for Land Girls. Here we see one of them at the controls of the combine harvester. St John's church is on the horizon to the left.

# Nine
# People

'The people make the place,' my father used to say, and he's right. People build the town, they live in it, and dictate its character. From a population of 2,000 in 1851 the town has grown steadily, with nearly 28,000 inhabitants in 1991. What follows is just a glimpse of how some of them spent their time over the years.

Harpenden Town football team around 1920 off to an away match in one of Read's charabancs. The man sitting by the middle door is George Gardner, who served either as secretary or treasurer of the club for thirty years. This is Amenbury Lane, Alfred Pratt's building is now Kitchens.

Miss Elizabeth Woodward wearing her wedding dress. In 1865 she married Peter Burgoyne, a cobbler at Southdown.

The Burgoyne family, *c.* 1898. Elizabeth is in the centre and Peter is wearing his cobbler's apron. The lady seated in the front is his mother.

The Rothamsted Ramblers ladies hockey team was founded in 1900 by Sylvia Creyke, granddaughter of Sir John Lawes. She is third from the left in the front row. The team wore navy blue skirts, white blouses and scarlet ties. They played on the Paddock at Hatching Green, which had been levelled for them by Mr Hodgson. It was the custom to have tea in the Institute on Southdown Road after games.

A young lady from Luton, visiting a friend in Harpenden around 1898. Cycling was very popular at the time. Note the strings protecting the rear wheel, designed to prevent her long skirt from being caught in it.

Cycling was still popular in the interwar years. Mr S.G. Llewellyn who lived above Lovibonds at Church Green had this model especially made in 1936 for family outings.

A photograph taken by a Harpenden schoolboy, *c.* 1907, in a field at Luton Hoo. Samuel Cody is carrying out an early flying experiment. He took off by running at full speed and managed, on this occasion, to remain airborne for a distance of thirty yards. Often confused with William Cody, Buffalo Bill, to whom he was not related, Samuel Cody was famous for his work on kites, and later on early aircraft.

An unknown young lady dressed for riding, *c.* 1905. Ladies rode side saddle in those days – riding astride only became popular after the First World War.

The Grand Harpenden Fair in 1923 was held to raise funds for the West Herts. Hospital at Hemel Hempstead which served the Harpenden area. The lower part of the Common was covered with a variety of stalls and amusements, including this chairoplane.

Another attraction was The Endeavour, a genuine coach from the pre-railway age. The building on the left is Abott and Anderson's oilskin clothing factory, rebuilt after a disastrous fire in 1916. On the right is the Old House, which in the nineteenth century was The Bull Inn, the sign of which is shown on page 2.

The skittle alley.

The fair had been so successful that another was held four years later. The fair's logo, used in advertising and on postcards, was a mounted highwayman.

The local knife grinder at work in 1930. He lived on the outskirts of Harpenden, and regularly wheeled his cart around the village.

J. Chalkleys' coal delivery cart in Sun Lane, *c.* 1910.

Salisburys' van in Coleswood Road in the early twenties. Their premises were at Kingston House in the High Street.

Abraham Saunders and Sons, removal contractors in Southdown Road, bought this Foden steam lorry in 1914 to supplement their fleet of horse-drawn vehicles. David Saunders is on the right while the man on the left is a salesman for Fodens.

A group of soldiers of the Notts. and Derbyshire Regiment (the Sherwood Foresters) photographed in Cravells Road where they were billeted in 1914. At the outbreak of war, over 4,000 men were stationed in Harpenden.

The Harpenden company of the Church Lads Brigade was founded in 1898, attached to St John's church. The Brigade was a Christian youth organisation and normally not so militaristic. But in 1914, when the photograph was taken, it was felt to be every man's duty to prepare himself for the war. Hence the training with (possibly dummy) rifles. Revd W. Colley, Captain of the Brigade, is seated third from left.

A military funeral in 1915, believed to be of a young soldier of the South Staffordshire Regiment who died of influenza. He was buried in St Nicholas churchyard with full military honours. Note the escort, marching with arms reversed. The civilian in front is Mr Frederick Piggott, the local undertaker.

At the end of the war, as part of its memorial, Harpenden opened the nursing centre at the bottom of Townsend Road. Here we see some of the prams at the baby clinic in the early thirties. The one on the left contains Joyce Ackroyd, daughter of the well known local baker and his wife, guarded by Mick, the family dog.

In the early years of the Second World War there was a national appeal for aluminium articles for use in aircraft production. A local ladies committee are showing part of their collection to Mr A. Rigby Fisher, Chairman of the Urban District Council, in the grounds of Harpenden Hall, in 1940.

Volunteer scrap collectors marching to the Public Hall with their spoils in 1942, led by the Chairman of the Urban District Council, Mr C.F. Putterill, and fellow Salvation Army bandsmen.

Two ladies from the British Legion making camouflage nets in rooms above the Harpenden Dairies in Station Road, *c.* 1942. Miss E.L. Busby on the left became Chairman of the Urban District Council in 1945.

Men of the wartime auxiliary fire service at the fire station in Leyton Road with their medium trailer fire pumps, *c.* 1941. These were designed to be towed behind private cars or vans and could be manoeuvred fairly easily over rough ground or debris.

Men of the Harpenden Home Guard on parade during a War Savings promotion week in the middle years of the Second World War.

A civil defence exercise in 1968 in Heath Road. The area was being cleared for new housing at the time, some of which can be seen on the left.

The Salvation Army Band was founded in 1912 by Mr C.F. Putterill, seated second from right. They are seen here outside their barracks in Amenbury Lane.

George Rodwell at the door of St Nicholas church in 1909. He had served the parish church as sexton, verger and parish clerk for nearly fifty years, having come here with Canon Vaughan, the first rector, in 1860, and was shortly to resign all his offices because of 'failing powers at an advanced age'. He was eighty-seven, and died three years later.

The Duke of Edinburgh made a private visit to Rothamsted in July 1954. He arrived by helicopter and, after coffee at the Manor House, visited all the various departments. He toured the farm on a tractor-towed trailer, sitting on a hessian covered bale of straw. He is talking to Mr B. Weston, the field superintendent.

Princess Margaret came to Harpenden on 6 April 1961 in her rôle as President of the Church of England Youth Council, to plant a tree on the site near Pickford Bridge, which was earmarked for the new All Saints church. She is seen at St Nicholas church with the rector, Revd Peter Bradshaw. Following them are Ernest Ackroyd, Chairman of the Urban District Council and Frederick Harris, clerk to the Council.

Morris dancing on Church Green in August 1953.

Harpenden swimming pool was opened on 7 May 1960 at a total cost of £20,000, a quarter of which had been raised by public subscription. Affectionately known as 'The Pool in the Park', its future as an outdoor pool is currently under discussion.

In 1937, to commemorate the Coronation of King George VI, the Harpenden Society erected the Harpenden sign on the Common. The Coat of Arms was designed by Frank O. Salisbury. Later, this stone panel was placed above the door of the new Public Hall, which was opened on 28 September 1938. The design did not conform to strict heraldic principles and was redrawn in 1949.

The Town Mayor's chain in 1995. There was, surprisingly, no chain of office for the Chairman of the Urban District Council until 1954. In that year Mr Sydney Shadbolt, who had organised two very successful festivals in the town, for the Festival of Britain in 1951 and the Coronation in 1953, left Harpenden. To mark his departure he presented this chain to the Council, with the redesigned Coat of Arms. Above it is an enamelled cameo, showing Mount Everest, to commemorate the fact that two Harpenden residents, Dr L.G.C. Pugh and Mr M.H. Westmacott, were members of the first expedition to climb it. The whole is surmounted by a crown, symbolising the Coronation of Queen Elizabeth II.

# Acknowledgements

I gratefully acknowledge the loan of photographs from:
Mr Noel Cantillon, editor of the *Herts. Advertiser*,
Mr Les Casey and the Harpenden Local History Society, Mrs Amy Coburn,
Miss I. Cooper, Mr Arthur Creighton, Mrs Marion Donaldson,
Mr A.W. Gray, Herts. County Record Office,
Mrs S. Jones, Professor Trevor Lewis of Rothamsted Experimental Station,
Mrs Joan Lovatt, Miss Ivy Lawrence, Mr S.G. Llewellyn, Mr A.J. Mann, Mrs M. Mardall,
Mr Eric Ogglesby, Mrs Joyce Nette, Mrs Anita Packe, Harpenden Town Clerk,
Mr John Savage, Mrs Mary Skinner, Miss J. Wade and Mr J. Whitelaw.
Thanks to Mr Chris Grabham, Luton Museum and the *Luton News* for permission
to reproduce Nos. 20B, 75, 83, 96A, 97A, 99 and 108B,
to Mr Geoff Woodward for the provision of much information,
to Mr Eric Meadows for permission to use some of his photographs,
and for copying most of the rest and to
Mrs Linda Goucher for transcribing my handwriting into a readable typescript.
Many of these pictures have been deposited with the Harpenden Local History Society
which is always glad to see any material of local interest.
Lastly, my apologies if anyone's name has been inadvertently omitted.